How Does a Hurricane Form?

by Megan Cooley Peterson

T0014870

Bullfrog Books

Ideas for Parents and Teachers

Bullfrog Books let children practice reading informational text at the earliest reading levels. Repetition, familiar words, and photo labels support early readers.

Before Reading

- Discuss the cover photo. What does it tell them?

- Look at the picture glossary together. Read and discuss the words.

Read the Book

- "Walk" through the book and look at the photos. Let the child ask questions. Point out the photo labels.

- Read the book to the child, or have him or her read independently.

After Reading

- Prompt the child to think more. Ask: Did you know about hurricanes before reading this book? What other kinds of storms would you like to learn about?

Bullfrog Books are published by Jump!
5357 Penn Avenue South
Minneapolis, MN 55419
www.jumplibrary.com

Library of Congress Cataloging-in-Publication Data

Names: Peterson, Megan Cooley, author.
Title: How does a hurricane form? / by Megan Cooley Peterson.
Description: Minneapolis, MN: Jump!, Inc., [2024]
Series: Science questions | Includes index.
Audience: Ages 5–8
Identifiers: LCCN 2022046850 (print)
LCCN 2022046851 (ebook)
ISBN 9798885244817 (hardcover)
ISBN 9798885244824 (paperback)
ISBN 9798885244831 (ebook)
Subjects: LCSH: Hurricanes—Juvenile literature.
Classification: LCC QC944.2 .P49 2024 (print)
LCC QC944.2 (ebook)
DDC 551.55/2—dc23/eng20230111
LC record available at https://lccn.loc.gov/2022046850
LC ebook record available at https://lccn.loc.gov/2022046851

Editor: Jenna Gleisner
Designer: Emma Almgren-Bersie

Photo Credits: Harvepino/Shutterstock, cover; Sergey Gordienko/Shutterstock, 1; andrejs polivanovs/Shutterstock, 3; kojihirano/Shutterstock, 4, 23tl; Alkan2011/Dreamstime, 5, 23br; lafoto/Shutterstock, 6–7; New Africa/Shutterstock, 8; Alberto Masnovo/Shutterstock, 9; Sven Hansche/Shutterstock, 10–11; Artsiom P/Shutterstock, 12; Elena11/Shutterstock, 13, 23bl; NASA images/Shutterstock, 14–15, 23tr; photo-vista.de/iStock, 16–17; Meindert van der Haven/iStock, 18–19; Robert Blouin/Shutterstock, 20–21; Krumao/Shutterstock, 24.

Printed in the United States of America at Corporate Graphics in North Mankato, Minnesota.

Table of Contents

Swirling Storm

The Sun shines on warm ocean water.

This heats the water more.
Some water turns to vapor.
We cannot see it.

vapor

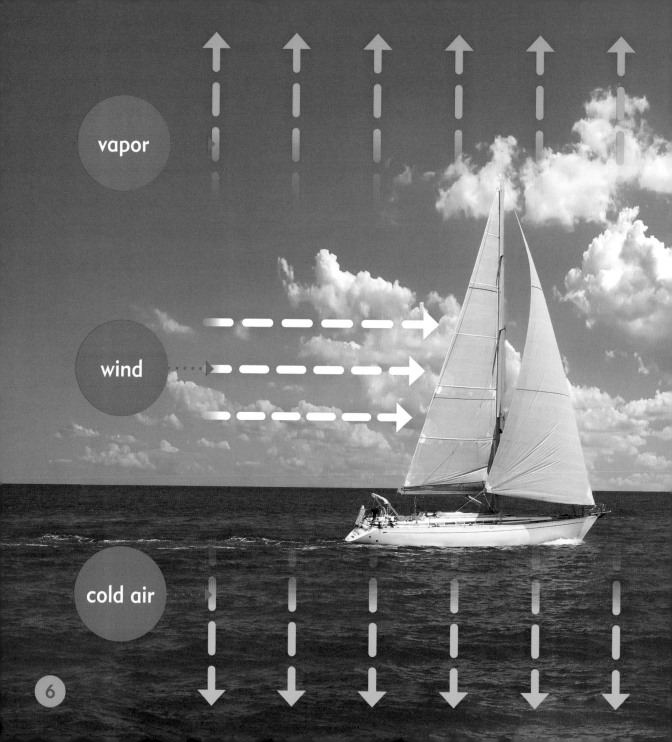

vapor

wind

cold air

6

Vapor rises.

Cold air sinks.

This makes wind.

Up high, vapor cools.
It turns into drops of water.

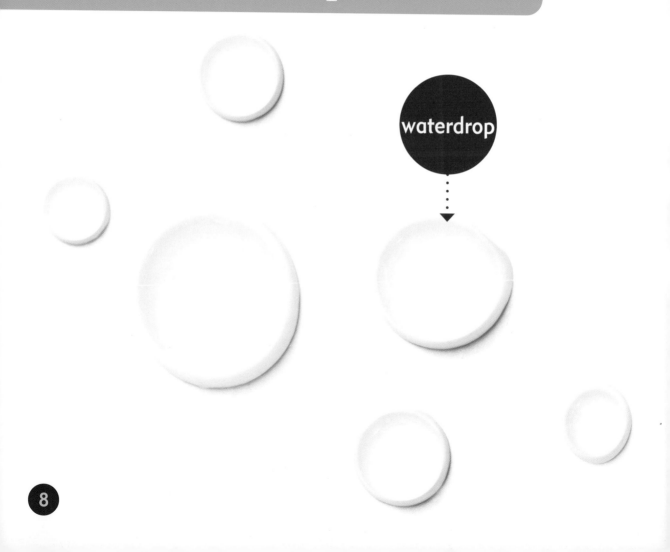

waterdrop

The drops make big clouds.

clouds

Rain falls.

Earth spins.
It pulls the wind.
This spins the clouds.

clouds

hurricane

The wind blows faster.

A hurricane grows.

The eye is the center of the storm.

There, it is calm.

The sky is clear.

eye

The storm hits land.
Waves crash.
Wind blows trees.
It rains.

On land, the storm slows.
Why?
It needs ocean water
to grow.

The storm is over.
We are safe.
We clean up.

How a Hurricane Forms

Hurricanes start over warm ocean water. How do they form? Take a look!

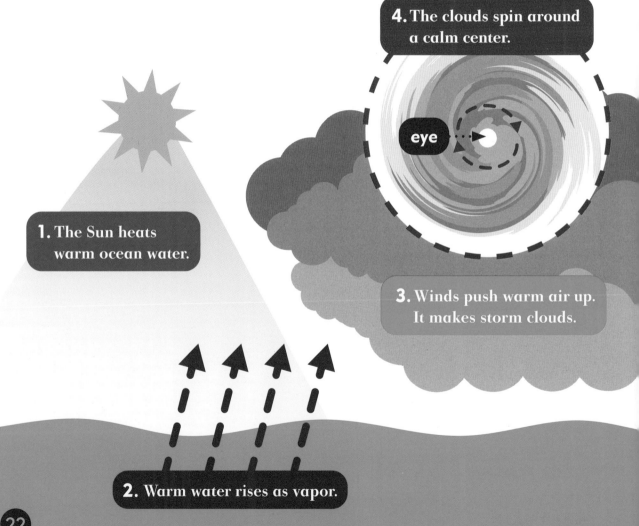

4. The clouds spin around a calm center.

eye

1. The Sun heats warm ocean water.

3. Winds push warm air up. It makes storm clouds.

2. Warm water rises as vapor.

Picture Glossary

calm
Peaceful and not troubled.

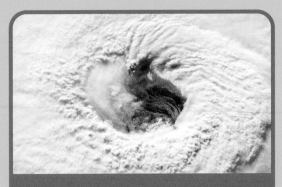

eye
The calm, clear area at the center of a hurricane.

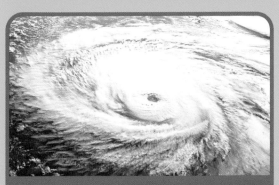

hurricane
A violent storm with heavy rain and high winds. A hurricane is also called a tropical cyclone.

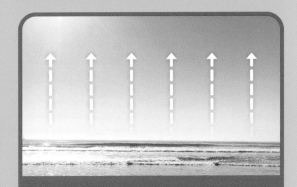

vapor
A gas made of drops of water mixed with air.

Index

To Learn More

Finding more information is as easy as 1, 2, 3.

❶ Go to www.factsurfer.com

❷ Enter "howdoesahurricaneform" into the search box.

❸ Choose your book to see a list of websites.